THE 1948 PALESTINE WAR

The Launch of Conflict in the Middle East

Written by Camille David
In collaboration with Mathieu Beaud
Translated by Carly Probert

THE PALESTINE WAR

KEY INFORMATION

- **When:** 15 May 1948 – 20 July 1949
- **Where:** In Israel and Palestine
- **Context:** Israeli-Arab conflict
- **Belligerents:** Israel against the Arab League, a coalition formed between Egypt, Iraq, Transjordan, Syria, Lebanon and Saudi Arabia
- **Commanders and leaders:**
  - Abdallah I, King of Jordan (1882-1951)
  - David Ben-Gurion, Israeli politician (1886-1973)
- **Outcome:** Israeli victory
- **Victims:**
  - Jewish camp: approximately 4 000 soldiers and 2 400 civilians dead
  - Palestinian camp: between 12 000 and 20 000 civilians and soldiers dead
  - Arab camp: approximately 4 000 soldiers dead

INTRODUCTION

A major contemporary conflict, the Israeli-Palestinian and Israeli-Arab tensions are still the source of front-page news. Between attempts at peace processes, failures in negotiations and terror attacks, the situation does not seem to be improving. The hostilities began in 1947 and took the form of several wars between Israel and several allied Arab States, in 1948 (Palestine War), 1956 (Suez Crisis), 1967 (Six-Day War), 1973 (Yom Kippur War), 1982 and 2006 (First and Second Lebanon Wars).

The first conflict, called the Palestine War or the War of Independence, followed the civil war (1947-1948) between the Jews and the Palestinians over the question of the territorial future of Palestine after the departure of the British forces, which had been the mandatory power in Palestine since 1922; the Jews, who had been arriving in mass in Palestine since the beginning of the 20th century, demanded the creation of an Israeli state, which the Palestinians opposed fiercely. The tensions between the two communities then continued to intensify. However, the situation evolved in favor of the Israelis and on 14 May 1948, the Zionist leader David Ben-Gurion proclaimed the independence of the Israeli State. The neighboring Arab countries then decided to invade Palestine, in order to put an end to the Zionist claims in the region. This is how the Palestine war began, in which the Jewish forces of Israel fought against a coalition made up of Transjordan, Egypt, Syria, and Iraq from May 1948 onwards and ended with the signing of the armistice at Rhodes on 24 February 1949.

POLITICAL AND SOCIAL CONTEXT

PALESTINE UNDER BRITISH MANDATE FROM 1922 TO 1948

Previously belonging to the Ottoman Empire, Palestine became a British protectorate in 1922.

While the outcome of the First World War (1914-1918) was still uncertain, the French and the British took part in the dismantling of the broad Ottoman Empire and signed the secret Sykes-Picot Agreement in 1916, which planned the division of the control over the Middle East between these two colonial powers. However, the League of Nations (international organization created at the end of the First World War in order to enforce international law and justice and put a stop to war) only officially gave Great Britain the necessary mandate to administer Palestine in July 1922. London was therefore required to deal with the difficult co-habitation involving the local Arab community and the Jews coming mostly from Europe and arriving in great numbers from the late 19th century. This immigration intensified at the beginning of the 20th century with the development of political Zionism.

GOOD TO KNOW

Zionism is a political movement advocating the creation of a Jewish State in Palestine. The Zionist demands, namely the desire to create a national Jewish homeland, were formulated by Austro-Hungarian jour-nalist Theodor Herzl (1860-1904) during the Congress of Basel in 1897, the movement's first international meeting. There, the territories of the Biblical Kingdom of Israel were chosen by the Jewish people who would thus be able to protect themselves from the rising antisemitism of the time. A Jewish National Fund was then created with the aim of purchasing land in that territory.

In 1917, the British Minister of Foreign Affairs, Arthur James Balfour (1848-1930), stated in a letter addressed to Baron Rothschild (1868-1937), the Vice President of the Jewish Knesset Committee, that the British Government intended to create a national Jewish homeland in Palestine, thus advocating a return of the Jews to their historic lands. Although this declaration generated the British support of the Zionist movement at first, the management of the region then forced them to consider the interest of the Arab inhabitants and the opinions of neighboring countries. In 1915, London had already promised independence and control of the territories that would be freed from Ottoman rule to the Egyptian King Hussein ibn Ali (c. 1856-1931), through the British High Commissioner of Egypt Henry McMahon (1862-1949). The Palestinian territories therefore became desireable objects.

The Jewish emigration towards Palestine grew even more during the thirties, and was reinforced by Adolf Hitler's accession to power and the enforcement of his anti-Jewish

politics: pogroms, stigmatization, ghettoization, depor-
tation and extermination generated a mass exodus. The
Jewish population in the territory amounted to 28% in 1940.
This important influx continued after the Second World
War (1939-1945), but not without difficulty: conflict, strikes
and hostilities erupted among the Palestinians between
1920 and 1947 and violence continued to grow between the
two communities. However, from 1945, the British opposed
the Jewish immigration more and more, as shown by the
Exodus affair: a ship, which was carrying 4 500 Jews, was
refused access to Palestine and brought back to France and
Germany.

Although tensions were mainly felt between Arabs and
Jews, incidents also broke out against the British colonial
power, culminating in the Great Revolt of 1936 to 1939,
an uprising that sought to establish an Arab Palestinian
nation, and was severely repressed by the Zionist militia.
In response to the uprising, Great Britain attempted to find
a solution by announcing a series of laws called the 'White
Paper' (1939), which advocated a unitary, independent
Palestine governed by the Arabs and the Jews, while
restricting Zionist immigration. The measures planned,
however, did not satisfy either of the two communities and
even provoked further incidents. In view of this new rise of
violence, the British attempted to resolve the problem. A
report proposing a modification of the 'White Paper' was
released in July 1946: it proposed a plan for the separation of
Palestine into two autonomous provinces whose collective
interests would be handled by a mandatory foreign power.
Nevertheless, disagreements persisted and a solution that

would satisfy both parties seemed unreachable. Moreover, as the process of decolonization began in the Middle East, the British announced their forthcoming withdrawal from Palestine on 18 February 1947. As the end of their mandate was scheduled for 15 May 1948, a special commission of the United Nations (UN) was put in charge of finding a solution to the problem of cohabitation.

The Great Revolt of 1936 to 1939.

A partition plan was voted on by the General Assembly of the UN on 29 November 1947, which abandoned the idea of a united state in favor of a binational state government. Thus, an Arab state and a Jewish state could coexist while the capital, Jerusalem (which would be given the status of international city) would be placed in the hands of the UN. The Jewish community in Palestine quickly accepted the proposed plan, as it corresponded to their expectations.

Conversely, the Palestinians and the neighboring Arab states refused to share the territory and therefore opposed both the plan and the creation of a Jewish state, which they believed would endanger Islam and the regional balance. They also refused the Jewish demands based on historical or religious references, and which they considered to be a form of colonialism orchestrated by the European powers and directed by the UN. Following this refusal, the tensions between the two camps grew even more intense and the civil war officially broke out on 30 November 1947.

THE CIVIL WAR OF 1947-1948

While the Palestinians wished above all to prevent the division of Palestine, the Jews wanted to secure the zone that had been given to them, even if this meant expelling the Arab populations who had settled there. Fighting broke out between the clandestine Jewish defensive militias such as the *Haganah*, the *Irgun* and the *Lehi*, and the Palestinian irregulars such as the *Jaysh-al-Jihad al-Muqaddas* – which can be translated as "army of the holy war" which was supported by Arab voluntaries who formed the Arab Liberation Army. The British forces, finding that they had lost enough men already, remained relatively passive in this civil war and tried to remain in the sidelines as they awaited the official date of withdrawal.

From January 1948, the Arab Liberation Army spread out in the coastal cities and strengthened its presence in Galilee (North of Israel) and Samaria (center of Palestine) while the men of the *Jaysh-al-Jihad al-Muqaddas* organized the blockade of 100 000 Jews in Jerusalem. An operation to resupply them was then put in place by the Israelis to help them, but the operation cost the lives of many men. Moreover, on the Palestinian territory, the circulation between the different Jewish zones, which were relatively far from each other, was difficult.

Although the Palestinians seemed to have the upper hand until the end of March 1948, the situation evolved in favor of the Israelis. However, the defeats of the *Haganah* cannot be put down to a weakness of the Jewish forces, but rather to a wait-and-see policy The reorganization of the army with regards to structure, training and equipment, namely thanks to the arrival of weapons from Czechoslovakia in April 1948, allowed them to launch victorious attacks on the Arab populations of the territories that they considered to be rightly theirs. Between early April and mid-May 1948, the Palestinian militias and Arab voluntaries were defeated.

During the last six weeks of the British mandate, the Zionist militias took control of the mixed regions, with the exception of Jerusalem – which they managed to resupply – and reestablished the communication between the Jewish zones. To do this, they applied the Plan Dalet, an operational plan of the *Haganah* dating back to March 1948 which, to ensure the territorial continuity of the future state of Israel, planned the destruction of the Arab villages and cities. This was the case, for example, with the villages of Haifa on 22 April, Jaffa on 13 May, etc. The plan also stated that in case of resistance, the armed forces must be destroyed and the population expelled from the Jewish state. Hundreds of thousands of Palestinians (between 700 000 and 750 000 people in total, according to certain sources) fled before the fighting or were chased away by the Jewish forces. They then followed the roads to Galilee or Samaria, or joined the refugee camps set up in the neighboring countries.

The exodus of Palestinians.

The many victories of the Jewish troops during the civil war led the Zionist leader, David Ben-Gurion, to proclaim the independence of the state of Israel on 14 May 1948, on the eve of the departure of the British. This was too much for the neighboring Arab countries, who did not accept this decision, and the next day, the Egyptian, Syrian, Transjordanian and Iraqi armed forces invaded the former mandated

Palestine in order to put an end to the Jewish demands. As for the Palestinian forces that had fought during the civil war, they were dissolved or absorbed by the Arab armies. Thus began an inter-state war, the Palestine War.

COMMANDERS AND LEADERS

DAVID BEN-GURION, ISRAELI POLITICIAN

Portrait of David Ben Gurion, 1949.

David Gruen, known as 'David Ben-Gurion', was an Israeli

politician, founder of the State of Israel and served as Prime Minister there from 1948 to 1953 and 1955 to 1963. He was one of the main defining figures of the history of Israel.

Born in Płońsk (Poland), David Ben-Gurion settled in Palestine at the age of 20, before being expelled by the Turks in 1915. Returning in 1917, he founded the first union of Israeli workers (*Histadrut*) in 1921, before becoming the general secretary of the Zionist Labor Party (*Mapai*). He also received the political responsibility for the *Yishuv* (term designating the Jewish community in Palestine at the time of the British mandate). As president of the Jewish Agency from 1935 onwards (one of the political organs in charge of the administration of the *Yishuv*), he also became the head of the *Haganah* armed forces, as it was under the control of the Jewish Agency.

It was he who refused the partition plans offered by the UN in 1947 and 1948, and he was responsible for the declaration of independence of the Hebrew state that same year. As Minister of Defense, he also led the Israel Defense Forces (*Tsahal*) which he created in 1984 from various armed groups. Supporting the soldiers' combativeness, he closely followed the military operations of the Israeli forces. This undisputed leader of the Jewish camp was behind all the important political and military decisions made by the Israeli state during the war.

In 1963, he retired from political life and died in Tel-Aviv in November 1973.

ABDALLAH I, KING OF JORDAN

Portrait of Abdallah I, King of Jordan.

Abdallah bin al-Hussein or Abdallah I of Jordan was born in Mecca in 1882. He became emir then King of Transjordan from 1921 to 1949, then King of Jordan from 1949 to 1951, when he was finally assassinated in Jerusalem by the Palestinian nationalists. He was the son of Hussein ibn Ali

(1916-1924), Sharif of Mecca, King of Hejaz (region located west of Saudi Arabia) and was one of the promoters of the Arab revolt of 1916 against the Turks. Abdallah I was at the head of Transjordan when it was under British mandate, and, despite the proclamation of its independence, Britain remained their only ally in the Middle-East during the Palestine War.

Before the beginning of the war in 1948, he received the honorary title of Supreme Commander of the Arab Liberation Army. The role he played during the Palestine War was significant: he was the leader of the most important army on the Arab side, the Arab Legion. His troops were on every front, even though they focused mainly on Cisjordan and Jerusalem. Aside from his military importance, Abdallah I had great political and diplomatic influence. His ambition was to create a great Arab state, the 'Greater Syria', which would include Transjordan, Palestine, Syria and Lebanon, and thanks to his well-trained armies, he had the means to make this dream come true.

His intentions regarding the Jewish states, however, were ambiguous: he claimed to oppose the creation of a Jewish state, but was mainly looking to prevent the creation of a Palestinian state, in order to acquire the territories himself. He wanted to annex Cisjordan, in accordance with a secret agreement concluded with the Israeli Minister of Foreign Affairs, Golda Meir (1898-1978). Indeed, this agreement stated that the Arab Legion would not fight Israel further than Cisjordan, once the territory had been captured. This region was claimed by Transjordan because there were nearly 70% of Palestinian people living there: Abdallah I wanted to add it to his country under the pretext that they were one same people. However, his territorial ambitions generated mistrust and dissensions inside the Arab camp, namely on the part of Syria and Egypt.

Because of his territorial ambitions, his military importance and his ambiguous attitude resulting from secret agreements, King Abdallah I was one of the most important figures on the Arabic side during the Palestine War.

ANALYSIS OF THE WAR

THE FORCES PRESENT

The Palestine War took place between Israel and the Arab countries, following the proclamation of independence of the Jewish state and the defeat of the Palestinians. The military forces present during the conflict were:

- On the Jewish side, the Army for the defense of Israel, called the *Tsahal*.
- On the Arabic Side, the Palestinian groups integrated into the neighboring armies (such as the *Jaysh al-Jihad al-Muqaddas*), the state armies (such as the army of Transjordan, the Arab Legion), those of Iraq, Egypt, Syria, Lebanon and Saudi Arabia, as well as the Arab Liberation Army, made up of volunteers and organized by the Arab League.

GOOD TO KNOW

Created on 26 May 1948, the army of Defense for Israel, or Israel Defense Forces, was called *Tsahal*. Before the existence of the Jewish State, the forces in charge of defending the Zionist people were the armed independent groups such as the *Haganah*, founded in the twenties with the aim to defend the Jewish emigrates against the potential Arabic attacks. This independent force was at the origin of the creation of the Israel Defense Forces and was joined in 1948 by other clandestine armies such as the *Lehi* and the *Irgun*.

During the Palestine War, the Arab Legion of Transjordan contained roughly 10 000 men divided into 4 legions and supported by 75 armored vehicles. Commanded by British officers, the army was experienced and well-equipped.

This war developed in several stages and included two periods of truce.

THE FIRST FIGHTS (MAY-JUNE 1948)

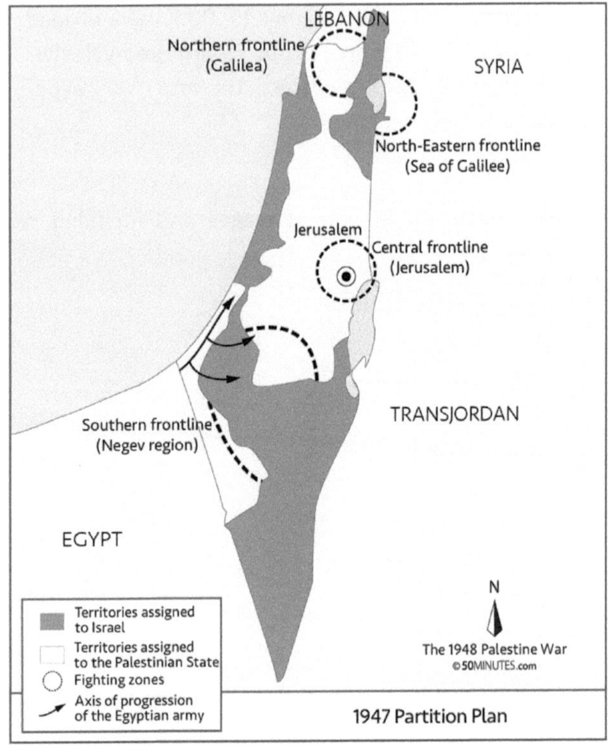

From 15 May to 11 June 1948, the Arab forces attacked following the proclamation of independence of the state of Israel:

- On the central front (around Jerusalem), which was the

most animated during the war, the Battle of Jerusalem was fought between the Israelis and the Transjordanian Arab Legion. Symbolically speaking, the capture of the Jewish neighborhood in the Old Town constituted a heavy loss. Unable to get there by force, the Transjordanian armies besieged the other Jewish neighborhoods of Jerusalem. Battles took place in surrounding villages - including Latrun - in order to supply the city with the arms, men and food necessary for the Israelis. These operations were also useful to maintain the communication channels between the regions they controlled. The Transjordanian troops were also concentrated in Samaria with the aim of taking political control of the region and annexing it. These troops were later relieved by Iraqi troops in some cities, which allowed them to focus on Latrun and Jerusalem.

- On the north-eastern front (around the Sea of Galilee) were the Syrian and Transjordanian troops, but the region remained comparatively quiet.
- On the northern front (located in Galilee), held by elements of the Arab Liberation Army, the territorial situation did not change significantly and the Israeli, despite their advantages in this region, did not manage to use them to strengthen their enclave in central Galilee and join up with Nazareth.
- On the southern front (located in the region of Negev), the Egyptian army met little opposition and deployed itself in three directions: along the coast (the current Gaza Strip), north of Negev and towards Judea where the low Jewish presence eased the deployment of the Egyptians as well as that of the Transjordanians, whose

expansionist ambitions concerned this region.

No decisive success resulted from this period, but casualties amounted to 1 600 for the Israelis (amongst which 1 200 were soldiers) and 1 400 for the Palestinians. From a territorial point of view, several cities and villages located beyond the partition plan were captured by the Israelis. Conversely, 12 Arab villages belonging to the Hebrew State were still escaping its authority. On 11 June, the two sides, exhausted, finally accepted the truce proposed on 22 May by the UN's mediator, Folke Bernadotte af Wisborg (1895-1948).

THE FIRST TRUCE (11 JUNE-8 JULY 1948)

The truce was accepted by the Israelis because they needed time to obtain the heavy weaponry bought in Europe, but also by Transjordan, which was satisfied with having reached some of its objectives. The other Arab countries first rejected the truce. Then, seeing their progress barred, they finally accepted a cease-fire. In order to prevent one of the camps from strengthening itself during that period, the UN declared an embargo on armament. However, Israel, which had secretly and illegally provisioned itself from the eastern bloc since 1947, managed to work around the embargo and obtain weapons from Czechoslovakia. The Hebrew state did not only enhance its military capacity but also reorganized its army for greater efficiency: its troops became stronger thanks intensive training. The Arab armies, as they depended materially on Great Britain, were unable to be resupplied.

In the meantime, the mediator Folke Bernadotte af Wisborg

established a new partition plan which gave Galilee to the Jews and Negev to the Arabs. However, the rejection of this project put an end to the truce and plunged the two camps into war once again 8 July 1948.

RESUMING THE FIGHT: THE TEN-DAY CAMPAIGN (8-18 JULY 1948)

Possessing the advantage of their more experienced troops, the Israelis changed their strategy by focusing more on the attack. Three operations were launched in ten days:

- The *Dani* operation was aimed at the center of the country and intended to secure and enlarge the passage between Jerusalem and Tel-Aviv. The cities of Lydda and Ramle were recaptured, whereas those of Latrun and Ramallah resisted. The recapture of Lydda gave way to a huge massacre (although this is denied by Israel today): 250 civilians were supposedly killed and almost 70 % of the inhabitants driven out.
- Operation *Dekel* took place in the north and was supposed to conquer Galilee in two stages. The first stage consisted of capturing the city of Nazareth, on 1 July, and the second involved capturing the villages surrounding the city. On 18 July, the Israelis occupied the whole of Southern Galilee.
- Operation *Kedem* aimed to regain total control over Jerusalem and above all, over the Old Town neighborhoods that had been taken by the Transjordanians. However, the city remained Jordanian until 1967 (Six-Day War);

SECOND TRUCE (18 JULY-15 OCTOBER 1948)

The Arabs were continually defeated, while the Ten-Day Campaign was considered a tremendous success for Israel. Faced with the urgency of the situation, the United Nations Security Council requested a new truce and the diplomats tried once more to come up with a partition plan that might satisfy all parties. Folke Bernadotte af Wisborg then presented his plan, which proposed:

- the annexation to Transjordan of the Arab zones, such as Negev and the cities of Lydda and Ramle;
- the occupation of Galilee by the Israelis;
- the instauration of international control over the coastal zone and Jerusalem;
- the repatriation of the Palestine refugees.

Such a plan clearly abandoned the idea of a Palestinian State. The Jewish state would now occupy Galilee while the passage between the coastal zones and Jerusalem would be under international control. As for the Palestinian refugees, they would be repatriated. This plan was also rejected, as the Arab countries, which still refused the existence of a Jewish state, did not want Transjordan to benefit from the situation by annexing the territories of the former Palestine. The Israelis thought this plan too unfavorable for them, and all the more so since they were in a position to win the war. After several threats, the UN mediator was assassinated by a small group issued from the Lehi on 17 September. He was then replaced by the American Ralph Johnson Bunche (1904-1971) who, instead of proposing partition plans, favored periods of cease-fire. On the day following the assassination, the last units of the *Yigurn* (although they were not involved) and those of the *Lehi* were dissolved in order to prevent terrorist actions and integrated into the *Tsahal*. The process of integration of the various militias into one big army, which had begun during the first truce, thus came to an end.

This second truce was again used by the Israeli army to strengthen its numbers and to operate reorganizations in order to improve the efficiency of its military forces. The weaknesses of the Arabs (problems with coordination, training and leadership), on the other hand, had not yet been resolved, which is why they found themselves at a true numerical disadvantage.

LAST RENEWED FIGHTING (15 OCTOBER 1948 – JUNE 1949)

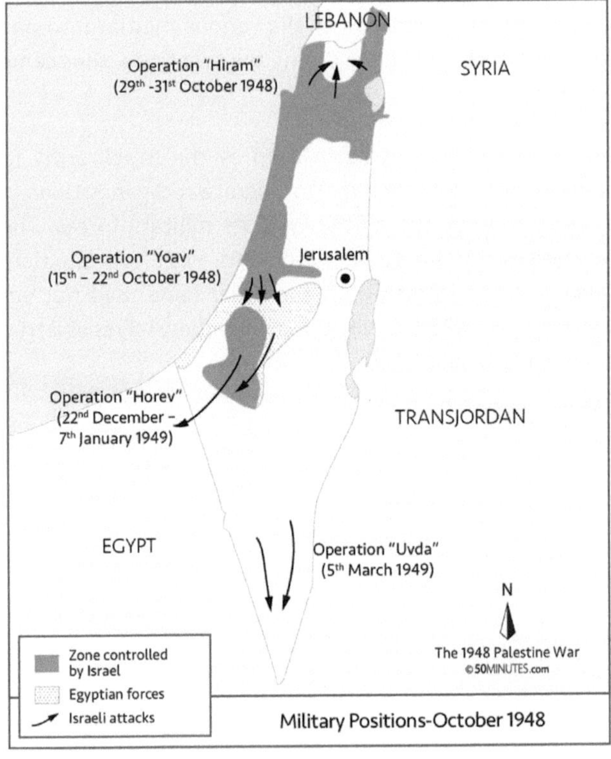

This period was defined by the strengthening of the Israelis' territorial domination in Palestine.

In the desert region of Negev, some Jewish settlings were surrounded by the Egyptian army, which prevented their annexation to the Jewish State. Operation Yoav, which consisted of breaking this encirclement and linking these various settlings to each other in order to create a territorial unity, was launched on 15 October 1949. An Israeli aerial attack placed the Egyptian in serious difficulty and provoked the intervention of the Arab Legion of Abdallah I. Instead of opening a second front, the Arab legion tried to fill the void created by the Egyptians who were retreating, so as to prevent their territory from being cut in two by an enemy attack. The Transjordanians thus extended their territories, as they also controlled Samaria (north of Cisjordan) and Judea (in the south). But on 22 October, a cease-fire was forced on them by international instances.

From 28 October, the Israelis attempted to recover the Arab enclaves that still escaped their control, yet seemed invincible, as they were defended by voluntaries of the of the Army of Liberation instead of by a State army. Taking advantage of the cease-fire with the Transjordanians and the Egyptians in Negev, the Jews concentrated their actions in that region and launched Operation Hiram, which enabled them to chase the men of the Liberation army towards Lebanon. The Israelis seized this opportunity to enter the Lebanese territory.

A second operation was launched on 22 December in the north of Negev. Thanks to Operation Horev, the Israelis invaded the territory of the current Gaza strip in order to create a diversion and to enable the discreet entrance of part of their forces in the south, near the Egyptian Sinai. However, this did not go unnoticed by the British, who then threatened to intervene as stated in their agreement with Egypt. The Israelis were thus forced to vacate the Sinai. The whole north of Negev remained in their hands, however, with the exception of an Egyptian pocket at Fagula, which still resisted and inflicted heavy losses on the Tsahal.

Operation Horev.

Throughout the rest of the region, the situation remained quiet during part of the Palestine War. As partition plans attributed this region to the Israelis, they did not consider them an absolute priority, especially since this long and narrow territory was stuck between the Egyptian and Transjordanian armies. While a cease-fire was signed with the Egyptians, the Transjordanians refused to do so: the Israelis then launched Operation *Uvda* on 5 March 1949. However, the aim of the Transjordanians was to maintain their presence, whilst keeping Cisjordan, and not to start another war against the Israelis. This is why they agreed to negotiate a cease-fire from January onwards and to retreat to Negev. Therefore, many consider the rise of the Israeli flag over the police station of Umm Rashrash on 10 March as the symbol of the end of the Palestine War.

The north-western region of Samaria, however, was controlled by the Iraqi and Transjordanian troops. As the Israelis wanted to concentrate their strength on the region of Negev, and then on Galilee, fighting had ceased in that region since the second truce. Moreover, Israel and Transjordan had drawn up a partial agreement on the division of territories in 1947, and as these were the two best armies taking part in the conflict, direct confrontation was a risk none of them were willing to take.

Negotiations (which were official from the end of February 1949 in Rhodes) then began concerning that territory: the Israelis wished not only for the departure of the Iraqi troops, but also for some villages between these two large zones, later called the 'Triangle'. Abdallah I of Jordan gave in to the demands of the Israelis and an armistice was signed on 30 March. The transfer of authority proceeded in a calm and orderly manner, and the Palestinian refugees present on the Jordanian territory were the only ones to be expelled. This was how Israel finally fixed the borders that would remain until 1967.

While the Iraqis refused to take part in the negotiations, the Rhodes agreements ended with the conclusion of four armistices signed in 1949: Israeli-Egyptian on 24 February, Israeli-Lebanese on 23 March, Israeli-Jordanian on 3 April and Israeli-Syrian on 20 July, the official date of the end of the Palestine War. The consequences of the Israeli victory were numerous.

Lebanon. The mistrust between countries should also be added, due to the ambiguous policies of some leaders, such as King Farouk I of Egypt (1920-1965), who said that he was ready to negotiate with Israel on the condition that he received the control of the Gaza strip, or Abdallah I, who secretly negotiated the annexation of Cisjordan. Therefore, these armies were under-equipped and under-trained and suffered from a lack of common strategy and tactical coordination between the different armed forces. This is why the Israelis, who were better prepared, won the Palestine War.

REPERCUSSIONS OF THE WAR

FAILURE OF THE LAUSANNE CONFERENCE

In addition to the armistice negotiations, the United Nations Conciliation Commission for Palestine organized the conference of Lausanne which took place from 27 April to 15 September 1949, in order to solve the problems born from the Israeli-Palestinian conflict. While the refugees asked for the authorization to return to the region where they used to live, Israel maintained its position and refused to modify its new borders. The attempts at conciliation failed once more.

TERRITORIAL CONSEQUENCES

The Rhodes agreements consecrated the territorial changes resulting from the Palestine War:

- The state of Israel took Galilee, from the coastal zone to Gaza, Western Jerusalem and the Negev region. The Israeli territory thus grew by a third compared to the territory initially allocated by the UN. The Israelis consequently possessed 77% of the territory instead of the 55% awarded by the 1947 partition plan. Indeed, 6 700 km^2 which should have belonged to the Palestinians was either annexed or occupied.
- The Gaza strip was governed by Egypt until 1967, when Israel reclaimed the territory;
- Transjordan, which took the name of Jordan, occupied Eastern Jerusalem and officially annexed Cisjordan on 24 April 1950, which then fell under Israeli control fol-

lowing the Six-Day War in 1967.

The idea of creating a Palestinian state thus seemed to have been abandoned and the UN validated the territorial changes without mentioning the initial partition plans again. However, none of the parties stated that they considered these borders to be definitive. They would be challenged several times and would cause further conflicts between Israel and its neighbors (Suez Crisis, Six-Day war, Yom Kippur War).

DEMOGRAPHIC CONSEQUENCES

The human losses were significant for each of the belligerents: 5 800 killed and approximately 12 000 wounded were declared on the Israeli side, 4 000 soldiers on the Arab side, and between 13 000 and 20 000 Palestinians. It is worth mentioning that these numbers vary significantly from one study to the other and that on the Palestinian side, the number of victims was never precisely recorded.

In addition to this heavy human cost, the war generated a massive exodus of approximately 700 000 Palestinians (sources vary from 530 000 to 900 000 refugees) who settled down mainly in Cisjordan, in the Gaza strip, in Lebanon and in Syria. The reasons behind these displacements were numerous: the violence of the fighting, the collapse of Palestinian society, the resignation of Palestinian leaders, and the departure of the political leaders, the expulsions by the Jews and the evacuation orders given by the Arab Higher Committee. This exodus is at the heart of the current issues of the Palestinian refugees, and was one of the main issues at stake in the Israeli-Arab and Israeli-Palestinian conflicts. As for the causes and circumstances of this exodus, they are still the subject of debate among historians. The opening of the Israeli archives in 1980 has allowed this question to be clarified, but debates are still open.

Consequently, with migrations, nationality changes caused by annexations (for instance, in Cisjordan, the inhabitants have adopted the Jordanian nationality) and the Palestinian diasporas into other countries, the population settlement of the region underwent deep changes.

POLITICAL CONSEQUENCES

The Arab states experienced considerable difficulties following the failure of the war and political regimes became unstable: the corruption and weakness of the armies were denounced. Consequently, many politicians were assassinated or overthrown: the Egyptian Prime Minister was assassinated at the end of December 1948, as was Abdallah I of Jordan on 20 July 1951. Meanwhile, the Syrian and Egyptian presidents were overthrown in coups d'état which took place in March 1949 and July 1952 respectively.

On the outcome of the conflict, the Israeli army identified itself as one of the main military powers in the region. Great Britain definitively left Palestine and the degradation of its relations with the Arab countries drove it to vacate the zones where it still had a military presence (Egypt, Iraq, and Jordan). In Israel, the *Mapai* Labor Party, which was already the favorite before the war, became even more popular, which allowed it to remain in power for the next thirty years, until the victory of the Likud (nationalist party) at the 1977 elections.

Consequently, the Palestine War was only the first in a long series of conflicts between Jews and Arabs. Nowadays, the situation between Israel and its neighbors is still tense and its conflictual relations with Palestine do not seem to have improved. Indeed, the two communities are still unable to see eye to eye about the questions of borders and the contiguity of their territories, nor on the matter of the refugees displaced during the conflict. There are also many litigious points such as the mutual acknowledgement of both people, the creation of a Palestinian state next to Israel, and the status of Jerusalem and the control of its holy places. The Israeli-Arab conflict still occupies an important place in the geopolitics of the Middle East, whose issues are still closely linked to the events of the Palestine War.

SUMMARY

1947
29th Nov.: Partition Plan of Palestine
30th Nov.: Beginning of the civil war

1948
14th May: Proclamation of
     the independence of Israel
15th May: Beginning of the Palestine War
11th June: First truce
8th July: Beginning of the Ten-Day Campaign
18th July: Second truce
15th Oct.: New Israeli operations

1949
24th Feb.: Signing the first armistice
20th July: Official end of the conflict
     Signing of the fourth armistice

- The Palestinian territory was under British mandate from 1922.
- Faced with the revolts of the local populations, the British scheduled their withdrawal for 15 February 1948.
- Tensions between Palestinians and Israelis intensified: each claimed the occupation of the territory, leading to an escalation of violence which culminated in the civil war of 1947 to 1948.
- On 14 May 1947, on the eve of the British withdrawal,

David Ben-Gurion proclaimed the independence of Israel, which triggered a military intervention of the neighboring Arab countries; thus began the Palestine war.

- The inter-state conflict was marked by two periods of truce, during which negotiations were triggered.
- The Israeli victories led to the signing of the armistice agreements of Rhodes, 24 February 1949, effectively ending this first war of the Israeli-Palestinian conflict.
- However, many issues were not solved and remain problematic today, such as territorial questions or the problem of the displaced populations.

We want to hear from you!
Leave a comment on your online library
and share your favourite books on social media!

FIND OUT MORE

BIBLIOGRAPHY

- Abitbol, M. (2005) *Juifs et Arabes au XXe siècle*. Paris: Perrin.
- CADTM (No date) *Le conflit israélo-palestinien: un siècle d'histoire en 15 minutes*. [Online]. [Accessed 5 December 2016]. Available from: <http://www.cadtm.org/IMG/pdf/historique_conflit_israelo-palestinien.pdf>
- Carré, O. (1991) *L'Orient arabe aujourd'hui*. Brussels: Complexe.
- Chaigne-Oudin, A.-L. (2010) Premier conflit israélo-arabe de 1948. *Les clés du Moyen-Orient*. [Online]. [Accessed 5 December 2016]. Available from: <http://www.lesclesdumoyenorient.com/Premier-conflit-israelo-arabe-de.html>
- Cordellier, S. (2005) *Le dictionnaire historique et géographique du XXe siècle*. Paris. La Découverte.
- Encyclopédie Larousse (No date) *David Ben Gourion* [Online]. [Accessed 5 December 2016]. Available from: <http://www.larousse.fr/encyclopedie/personnage/David_Gruen_dit_David_Ben_Gourion/98857>
- *L'Histoire du monde: Le monde en guerre, de 1940 à 1959* (1993) Paris: Larousse.
- Pappé, I. (2000) *La guerre de 1948 en Palestine. Aux origines du conflit israélo-arabe*. Paris: La Fabrique.
- Venayre, S. (No date) Indépendance d'Israël, proclamation de l'(1948). *Encyclopædia Universalis*. [Online]. [Accessed 5 December 2016]. Available from: <http://www.universalis.fr/encyclopedie/

proclamation-de-l-independance-d-israel/>

ADDITIONAL SOURCES

- Gelber, Y. (2006) *Palestine 1948: War, Escape and the Emergence of the Palestinian Refugee Problem*. Eastbourne: Sussex Academic Press.
- Gresh, A. and Vidal, D. (2004) *The New A-Z of the Middle East*. London: I. B. Tauris & Co Ltd.
- Morris, B. (1987) *The Birth of the Palestinian Refugee Problem (1947-1949)*. Cambridge: Cambridge University Press.
- Morris, B. (2001) *Righteous Victims: A History of the Zionist-Arab Conflict, 1881-1999*. New York: Random House Inc.
- Morris, B. (2009) *1948: A History of the First Arab-Israeli War*. London: Yale University Press.
- Morris, B. (2010) *One State, Two States: Resolving the Israel/Palestine Conflict*. London: Yale University Press.
- Rogan, E.L. (2008) *The War for Palestine: Rewriting the History of 1948*. Cambridge: Cambridge University Press.

ICONOGRAPHIC SOURCES

- The Great Revolt of 1936 to 1939. Royalty-free reproduction picture.
- Exodus of Palestinians. Royalty-free reproduction picture.
- Portrait of David Ben Gourion, 1949. Royalty-free reproduction picture.
- Portrait of Abdallah I, © Cecil Beaton.

- Operation Horev. © Nadav Man Collection.

FILMS AND DOCUMENTARIES

- *Exodus.* (1960) [Film]. Otto Preminger. Dir. USA: Otto Preminger Films, Carlyle Productions.
- *Cast a Giant Shadow.* (1967) [Film]. Melville Shavelson. Dir. USA: Batjac Productions, Bryna Productions.
- *Kedma.* (2002) [Film]. Amos Gitai. Dir. Israel: Agav Hafakot, Arte France Cinema, BIM Distribuzione, MK2 Productions, MP Productions, R&C Produzione.
- *Ô Jérusalem.* (2006) [Film]. Élie Chouraqui. Dir. France: Les Films de l'Instant.
- *The Sons of Eilaboun.* (2007) [Documentary]. Hisham Zreiq. Dir. Germany/Palestine/Israel.

IMPROVE YOUR GENERAL KNOWLEDGE
IN A BLINK OF AN EYE !

www.50minutes.com

www.50minutes.com

Ebook EAN: 9782806272959

Paperback EAN: 9782806272966

Legal Deposit: D/2015/12603/617

Cover: © Primento

Digital conception by Primento, the digital partner of publishers.